GW00459813

SEO 101

Learn the Basics of Google SEO in One Day

By Steven "SEO" Samson

Table of Contents

Copyright 2015 by Steven Samson - All rights reserved.

This document is geared towards providing exact and reliable information in regards to the topic and issue covered. The publication is sold with the idea that the publisher is not required to render accounting, officially permitted, or otherwise, qualified services. If advice is necessary, legal or professional, a practiced individual in the profession should be ordered.

- From a Declaration of Principles which was accepted and approved equally by a Committee of the American Bar Association and a Committee of Publishers and Associations.

In no way is it legal to reproduce, duplicate, or transmit any part of this document in either electronic means or in printed format. Recording of this publication is strictly prohibited and any storage of this document is not allowed unless with written permission from the publisher. All rights reserved.

The information provided herein is stated to be truthful and consistent, in that any liability, in terms of inattention or otherwise, by any usage or abuse of any policies, processes, or directions contained within is the solitary and utter responsibility of the recipient reader. Under no circumstances will any legal responsibility or blame be held against the publisher for any reparation, damages, or monetary loss due to the information herein, either directly or indirectly.

Respective authors own all copyrights not held by the publisher.

The information herein is offered for informational purposes solely, and is universal as so. The presentation of the information is without contract or any type of guarantee assurance.

The trademarks that are used are without any consent, and the publication of the trademark is without permission or backing by the trademark owner. All trademarks and brands within this book are for clarifying purposes only and are the owned by the owners themselves, not affiliated with this document.

Introduction

I want to thank you and congratulate you for purchasing the book, *"SEO 101: Learn the Basics of Google SEO in One Day"*.

This book has actionable steps and strategies on how to master Google SEO.

If you know a little bit on how the Internet works, you probably understand that being on the first page of Google or any other search engine for a particular popular keyword (keyword phrase) ultimately means money in your pocket. It doesn't matter whether you are running a blog where you collect emails or are running an online store; if you are on the first page for a certain keyword, you get a ton of leads, which means that the likelihood of having more conversions is even higher.

Think of it this way; I'd like to compare your website to a jewelry shop. If you rank highly on the search engines for a certain keyword related to jewelry, you could think of your store as one of the most pronounced jewelry stores in a street where all stores in the area sell jewelry. Well, the problem is that every other site in your niche has a similar goal. This means that you must be outstanding in getting your site to be attractive in the eyes of the search engines and in the eyes of those who visit your website. This is the essence of SEO. Certainly, SEO is a complex topic that many website owners want to ignore. However, this doesn't make it impossible to learn. With this comprehensive guide, I will teach you everything you need to know about Google SEO.

Thanks again for purchasing this book, I hope you enjoy it!

Mastering The Basics: Why Is SEO Important?

Search Engine Optimization or "SEO", plays a major role in determining how much traffic each crawled and indexed website gets. Unfortunately, the practice of SEO changes every day. As any SEO-savvy, webmasters will tell you: Google and other search engines are constantly innovating and implementing new ranking factors geared towards providing their users with exact matches for their searches and the best user experience (a webmaster in this case could mean a person with a blog/website or a company with an online presence).

Ranking first on Google takes a lot of concerted effort with SEO forming a very big part of these efforts. To make the matter worse, Google ranking factors change almost on a daily basis as Google strives to offer its users the best user experience possible.

Here is the thing though; SEO does not have to be rocket science. In fact, even though Google and other search engines do not explicitly state their ranking factors, with a little SEO effort and work, your website could rise up the ranks to number one on Google in very little time.

Search Engine Optimization 101

As you already know, SEO stands for search engine optimization. Search engine optimization is the process of ensuring that a website is friendly to search engines in order to generate organic search traffic thus driving more exposure and profits for any online business. A lot goes into website optimization. Nevertheless, the whole practice of SEO works towards ensuring that the search engine spiders (virtual robots that periodically grab websites for indexing) over at Google and other search engines can relate your website or website content to the queries users are typing into their search bars when searching for information.

Note: These queries are called KEYWORDS. Keywords form a very important part of SEO. We shall look at some of these later.

To someone who has little or no SEO experience, this understanding may seem vague and indifferent. Let's back track a bit.

What exactly is SEO?

SEO as we know and understand it means any changes, tweaks, or actions you may make to a webpage or content to influence that site's page or content rank on a search engine. The discipline of SEO covers many things. For example, one of the most fundamental parts of being great at SEO is an understanding of how to find easy-to-rank for keywords and how to integrate these keywords in your web content for easier visibility and indexing by the search engines (more on keywords and content a bit later).

Another great example of SEO practice is back linking (one of the key aspects search engines use to index pages). As you can see, SEO encompasses many areas. In fact, if you own an online business or intend to start one, the one thing you must know is that SEO is everything:

- It is the words on your page or content

- It is how these words interact with their intended users and how they interact with the search engines

- It is how user friendly your website is

- How helpful it is to visitors

- How many other sites are linking back to your site, and how well structured it is for crawling.

Coincidentally, SEO determines how successful your online business is because it determines how much organic traffic your website generates. A huge percentage of internet users start their online search at a search engine. This makes SEO one of the most important tools to have in one's arsenal. So why is SEO so important?

Why Is SEO So Important?

As indicated, websites generate traffic in different ways. Nevertheless, organic traffic accounts for a large part of all website traffic. Don't get me wrong; other methods of content marketing such as social media marketing are also effective traffic sources for most websites. However, if you own a website, you can testify to the fact that most of your website traffic is organic. Any webmaster understands that good SEO equals to organic traffic, which is equal to online success.

If we're being honest, the importance of SEO is a very personal thing to most of us. In fact, how important SEO is to you largely depends on your online goals. For example, do you want to optimize your site or content for traffic conversion purposes or do you simply want to get some eyeballs on your content?

Now, as you may have guessed, SEO is central to most websites online success. Although SEO holds special meaning and importance to each webmaster, let us examine 3 reasons why SEO is so important.

Reason 1: Visibility and Branding

As we indicated, most people start a huge percentage of their online journey at a search engine search-bar. In fact, if you're being completely honest with yourself, most of your online products and service purchases start at a search engine. As you can see, SEO, i.e. optimizing your website to ensure that it appears first (or at the very least, the first 3 spots on SERP (search engine results page) plays a very important role in website and brand visibility.

Other than visibility, a first page appearance for specific keywords or terms related to your content can also be good for business. For example, if you're targeting the online business niche (a niche is a segment of a market), by being first on Google, if your website is helpful and friendly to the visitors and Google, placing first can increase your conversion if your website is affiliated with specific products or if you sell your own products. This is especially useful because as you may know, most people don't just search once, they search, look through the results, refine their search criterion and search again.

Therefore, if you can optimize your pages and content for specific keywords and appear first for all variations of those specific keywords, you can bet your website and brand will be visible to thousands of internet users and because these users trust Google to give them matches closest to their search, your brand trust rating will skyrocket.

Reason 2: Credibility and more business

Credible brands are often the most visible brands. In fact, most users make a point of noting which companies or websites show up on SERP for specific keywords. To most of these users, the fact that Google, one of the most trusted search engines, gives you a first place listing on SERP translates into a vote of confidence. While this may seem a bit exaggerated, as research shows, higher rankings are equal to more credibility in the eyes of the consumers.

More credibility is equal to more traffic. Traffic is the first step in the conversion triangle. Although a first placement on Google does not automatically translate into more sales for your business, first placement means more eyeballs on your website and content. Further, if your content or website is relevant to the search term, and helpful to the target audience, it's unquestionably clear that some of these visitors will become your customers. Think of a Google first placement as a brick and motor on one of the busiest streets.

Reason 3: Highest ROI

Not every webmaster uses SEO for profit marketing purposes. However, as a marketing strategy, SEO has the highest return on investment in any marketing or advertising scenario. SEO is an inbound marketing strategy. This means that it allows a webmaster to market a website/product or content to target audiences searching for that specific product, service or content.

This means that people searching for specific content or products related to your website have one goal: to find the most relevant search result. SEO is unlike a TV ad where an ad interrupts a user. SEO allows you to present specific target audiences with results and information that matches their exact searches.

SEO is a multi-discipline endeavor. Nevertheless, at its core, it's a traffic generation strategy. SEO gets you in front of potential customers looking for exactly what your website or company may be offering.

As we also indicated earlier, SEO is not one discipline per se: it is many aspects of search engine optimization coming together in perfect unison to ensure that your website/content appears for relevant keywords.

With a better understanding of what SEO is, and its importance, I would say we are ready to look at various facets of SEO and understand how we can use each of these elements to increase our search rankings.

On-Page Optimization

As we have already seen, there are many reasons why SEO is such an important part of digital marketing and why digital marketers are always looking for SEO strategies guaranteed to give them a first place on SERP placement.

As we have also seen, SEO includes many areas. One of these keys areas is on-page optimization.

What Is On-Page Optimization?

On-page optimization is any direct webpage/content changes you may make to increase website visibility or ranking.

On-page optimization forms one of the key facets of SEO. Doing proper on-page optimization could mean the difference between SERP nirvana and the SEO doghouse.

Why is OPO so important?

If we're being honest, SEO in general falls into two main divisions: on-page and off-page SEO. On-page SEO is anything you do on-page, i.e. any direct changes you may make to a website or piece of content on page. This may include the creation of search engine/user friendly, keyword optimized content, keyword research, and targeting, customizing your URL with keywords, using META tags, etc.

Think of on-page SEO in terms of a skyscraper foundation. If your on-page SEO is poor or wanting, you can bet that anything else you do off-page (anything else you put on top of the foundation), will have zero positive effects on your ranking. This means that without good on-page optimization, any off-page optimization you undertake may be an effort in futility. Every serious digital marketer with a need for traffic must understand this.

Other than being the foundation, there are other reasons why on-page SEO is important. Let us examine some of these reasons.

On-page SEO is the search engine language and the User's language too.

Which of these two situations do you think is easier and much better at helping you rank: shoddy on-page SEO with a ton of Off-page SEO work, or off-page SEO built upon great on-page SEO? If you answered the latter, congratulations; you understand the importance of on page SEO.

Although it may not seem like it, search engines and search engine spiders are computer programs. They only understand computer languages. When you get your On-page SEO right, you use this computer language to inform search engines the scope of your entire site, i.e. what your website is all about.

Moreover, on-page SEO is as much about the search engines as it is about the user. Google, the biggest search engine by number of searches, clearly states that one of their ranking criteria is how helpful your site is to the users.

Quick note: Page ranking and search ranking criteria has come a long way. Long gone are the days when ranking first on Google or other search engines depended on how many keyword you stuffed on your website. Today, although keywords play a very important role in SEO, it is not about how many keywords you use; it is about where you place them, and how well you integrate them into your helpful content. Today, search is all about providing quality to the end user. This is the goal of search engines. It should be yours too.

On-page SEO covers about 80% of everything you must do to rank

On-page optimization covers about 80% of what you must do to rank on Google. It covers areas such as quality content, how well you integrate keywords into your content how many times the keywords appear and where they appear, Meta description, how you link to other quality sites, Meta titles, etc. As you can see, these are all things that determine how Google ranks pages.

If you build your website on faulty On-page SEO, you are building your online business or website on a faulty foundation. What is so unfortunate is that despite its importance and ease of implementation, many website owners still get on-page SEO wrong.

I know that when I say on page SEO is easy, you might be very skeptical. Let's recap: On page SEO covers the quality content you create (remember quality content is about providing value to the audience), it covers the keywords you target and how you use them on your website.

Easy On-page optimization Guide

How well you optimize your page is one of the key factors Google uses to organize the web aka rank pages in accordance with their relevance to the user searches and how user friendly the page is.

To speak the language of search engines, get your On-page SEO right, and rise up the ranks to page one, pay attention to the following:

<u>Content</u>

Content is the most important part of On-page SEO.

Unfortunately, there is a divide on what makes great, SEO friendly content? Let's settle the score here. Great content is original. This means that your content is not plagiarized from another site. It means content that includes text description for non-text items such as video and images (alt attribute), content that adds value to the target audience. For example, if someone types "how to cure acne naturally" goes through to Google, looks at SERP results, and lands on your page, your content should answer their question. It also means content that is well-researched.

Note: Research shows that longer posts rank better on Google

Formatting, Titles, and Descriptions

When Google spiders get to your page, they first scan your page titles (Meta title), headings, descriptions (Metadescriptions), images (alt attribute), etc. Crawling robots do this so that they can determine what your website is all about (so that they can relate it to user searches), authority, content, etc. and then use that information to place your website at a certain position on their index.

When creating pages, ensure that each page has a unique title relevant to the keywords you're targeting. This means that if you're creating a page or publishing a post, ensure that the titles and permalinks are keyword customized.

For example; If you aim to rank for "natural acne cures', a page with the following permalink URL: *yourpage.com/=123* would not rank better than a page with the following URL: *yourpage.com/=naturalacnecures.*

The same rule applies to all your content and pages. For example, if we were to write content for the above, our SEO optimized blog title would look like *yourpage.com/5-natural-acne-cures-you-should-try-right-now.*

Note: Google has stated that their crawling spiders pay special attention to the first three words of any content or page. Make sure to place your keywords first.

Description also includes the information you fill out in the Meta description. The Meta description is the page description users see on their search engine results page. When creating your Meta description, make it descriptive and make a point of using the keywords you intend to rank for as long as it does not compromise on readability. Your Meta description should not be more than 155-160 characters because search engines truncate anything above that.

In terms of formatting, ensure that your page load speed is in the red (use Google pagespeed to check your page load speed). Formatting also means formatting your content using the H1 H2 H3 and H4 tags, highlighting important parts of your content in bold and italic.

Formatting also means optimizing your images. Smaller image sizes equal faster page load time. You should also ensure that any non-text content on your website also has a descriptive alt tag related to the keywords you aim to rank for. Also, ensure that your images have appropriate titles. For example, instead of having image1.jpg, you can have cureacnenaturally.jpg. Ensure that all your pages are grouped into categories to help search engines and users find your content without a lot of hassle.

Interlinking and keyword optimization

Ensure that all your pages are keyword optimized. This means including keywords in all the strategic areas we have looked at (title tag, Meta tag, alt description, first 100 words of your content, <H> tags, etc.).

This means doing proper keyword research before using keywords on your content. Pay heed to keyword density without stuffing your keyword. Instead of stuffing keywords, use related keywords and synonyms.

Another key factor Google uses in their ranking is bounce rate. A bounce rate is the minimum amount of time a user spends on your website. A high bounce rate tells Google that users don't spend a lot of time on your page. Through this, Google assumes that the reason users are not spending a lot of time on your content is that it's not helpful to their search queries.

To decrease your bounce rate, you should build internal links to helpful content on your site. In this respect, when interlinking, use good, keyword optimized anchor text.

Recap: When doing your on page optimization, ensure that your Meta title, title tags, Meta description, keyword, content word count, <H> tags, alt attributes, permalinks, and all other accessibility features are completely optimized.

Now that we have covered everything on page SEO, let us look at another key ranking factor: Site-wide optimization.

Site-Wide Optimization

Site-wide optimization is the more technical side of SEO. It focuses on eliminating all site wide elements that may affect how a website appears to Google and the target audience. It focuses on issues such as indexing issues, usability issues, structural issues, etc.

What's All The Fuss About Site Wide Optimization?

Although search engines are extremely clever, they are still computers. Search engines cannot read a few things. For example, for search engine spiders to index your page, they first scan it.

They do this to understand what your site is all about, relate it to user searches, and then give it a number on their index depending on how relevant it is to the search query, how user friendly it is, how optimized it is, etc.

Unless you use alt tags on your images and other non-text media, Google spiders cannot read them (that is why naming your media appropriately and using keywords on the alt attributes is important).

Like SEO, site-wide optimization is many things. For example, site-wide optimization is optimizing all your images and other media to ensure the best page load speed. It is also creating structured links that don't return errors. It may also be coding optimization and URL optimization.

Side wide optimization focuses on the key elements of a website. For example, when creating your awesome content, you undoubtedly use media. However, images and videos are some of the major factors that influence page load speed, a key ranking factor. By doing site wide image and media optimization, you can easily ensure that the media not only adds value to your content, but it also adds value to your rankings in that it allows you a chance to explicitly tell search engines what your website is all about.

As we have indicated, like SEO, site-wide optimization is many things. This should not scare you. Site wide optimization is easy once you understand what to look out for. Let us look at some of the things you should pay attention to when doing your site wide optimization.

Site Wide Optimization Tips And Tricks

There are many ways to do site wide optimization. In fact, most marketers will be quick to tell you that site wide optimization often varies from one website to the other. Here are a few things should do to ensure that your website is well optimized.

Create a linking strategy

A linking strategy refers to all inbound and outbound links on your site (more on linking a bit later). Create a linking strategy ensures that a user can jump to any page published on your website from any page on your site. For example, if a user visits *yourwebpage.com/5-natural-acne-cures-you-should-try-right-now*, from that page, they should be able to jump to any other location on your website.

Make navigating your site easy for users and for search engines

Navigation is one of the key factors search engine use to index the web. You want to make sure that your site is easy to navigate with no broken links or errors. Ensure that a user can jump from one location to the other from any area of your website and make sure that your website features a sitemap.

A site map is a logical list of all pages and content on a website. Your site should have a HTML sitemap for users and a XML sitemap for search engines. Most websites today have a sitemap link at the footer.

A site map makes it easier for search engines to navigate through your website; it also makes it easier for users to navigate through your webpage. This increases usability, which is a key ranking factor.

Fortunately, most content management systems (CMS) like WordPress and others have tools such as Yoast SEO plugin for WordPress that makes it easy to create a sitemap.

Another navigational factor you should pay attention to is creating easy to understand menus that make navigating your site easier. For example, if you use WordPress to manage your content/website, you should ensure that your homepage has all relevant menus pointing to specific segments of your website.

Another site wide navigational feature you should pay proper attention to is ensuring that all your content is grouped into categories. For example, if you use WordPress, you can create a category menu for your 'how to' articles and place that somewhere strategic on the navigational bar.

Get your keywords game right

Keywords play a very important role in search engine optimization. As we indicated earlier, the days when keyword stuffing worked are long gone. Today, getting your keyword game right means ensuring that your keywords are placed in all the strategic positions (title tags, Meta tags, etc.,) and they integrate well into the awesome content.

Keywords are the foundation of all traffic coming to your site. If you fail to get keyword research right, it is very unlikely that your website will outperform other sites on SERP. For example, one-word keyword phrases like 'acne' or 'money' are harder to rank for than multiple word phrases like "'natural acne cures' or 'how to make money online'.

Ideally, unless you have a high traffic authority site, target easy to rank for. This strategy is especially helpful when your aim is to outdo your competition and rank for lower competition keywords. Again, in terms of keywords, one of the key things you should consider is having keywords in all the right and strategic places we mentioned earlier, i.e. keywords on the permalink, titles, Meta tags and description as well as other strategic locations such as outbound links.

Capitalize on analytics

Analytics allow you to know where your users are coming from, where they are going once they get to your site, and how long they are staying on your site. Analytics play a very huge part in SEO and it is thus a very important SEO must do. Fortunately, Google analytics is very easy to set up.

Utilize static pages

If your site has many dynamic pages, more so if your page has a lot of duplicate content, consider converting your content into static pages. Moreover, if your homepage content changes constantly, consider leveraging on a static homepage to store information that does not change but that points to other locations on your site. This is especially useful considering that an index page with content that changes constantly has a negative SEO effect.

Get your content game right

We shall not tire from stating it: content is bread and butter. Content is the whole reason websites are ranked. You have to realize that Google wants to provide the most relevant searches for their users. Therefore, to rank better, your content has to be out of this world. Out of this world in that although it may be optimized for search engines, it is not written for search engines but for humans.

Remember, it is easier to rank well-thought out content with minimal SEO work than it is to rank bad content with a ton of SEO work.

Site wide optimization is all about fixing any site-wide feature that may affect ranking or indexing. As indicated earlier, Site wide optimization is a bit technical. This should not scare you. With the use of a tool such as Google Page Insights, it is easy to analyze your site for site-wide optimization factors that may affect your overall website performance.

Keyword Research

Anyone who has been in the SEO scene for a while will be quick to point out that keyword research is perhaps one of the most important aspects of SEO.

All searches start with keywords. In fact, without keywords, there would be no need for search engines. What exactly is a keyword?

What exactly is a keyword?

Keywords are the search terms users type into their search engine search-boxes when searching for information. For example, if we go with our acne example, *"how to cure acne naturally'* is a keyword. This is because it is something someone looking for acne cures would type into their search bar.

Keywords form a very big and important part of SEO. Think of them as the Mr. Atlas to your earth: they support and determine how much traffic your website generates. They support your online universe.

Keywords fall into different categories.

Types of Keywords

Keywords often dictate the type of content you create for your website. For example, if you have an acne website, it does not make sense to target a high competition, single word keywords such as 'acne' because it is likely to be very competitive and hard to rank for. On the other hand, a keyword such as "natural holistic acne cures" is less competitive.

Generally, there are three main types of keywords.

Type 1: Generic Keywords

Generic keywords are generic in nature. This means that they are very unspecific and not related to a specific niche. For example, a search term such as "money" or "shoes" is very generic and unspecific because the person searching for the above terms could be searching for the meaning of money or shoes, or they could be searching for how to make money or where to find specific type of shoes.

Generic keywords are often very short and have multiple users searching for them on a daily basis. Generic keywords are often very competitive and broad.

Broad Match Keywords

Broad match keywords are a step up from generic keywords. Broad match searches are often very specific. For example, a broad match keyword for money would be 'make money freelancing' or make money trading forex". Broad match keywords will often drive targeted traffic to your site with not as much competition as generic keywords.

Long Tail Keywords

Long tail keywords are akin to sentences that user's type in their search boxes. An example of a long tail keyword could be *"how to set up an affiliate marketing website that makes money"*

Lon tail keywords are very specific and the users that type them into their search boxes are often looking for very specific information. Although long tail keywords do not always have the most user searches, ranking for a long tail keyword can drive a lot of targeted traffic to your website.

Now that we have looked at some of the major keyword categories, you may be wondering, "Why are keywords so important?" If you were wondering, here are a few reasons why keywords and keyword research is such an important part of SEO.

Why is Keyword Research so Important?

Although Google does not explicitly state that keywords are one of their key ranking factors, keywords play a very central role in user searches and thus ranking and indexing.

Google's work is to provide users with the most relevant results according to their searches. Google cannot know what your site or content is about unless you tell it by placing keywords in all the strategic locations we delved into earlier.

Keyword importance largely varies from one webmaster to the other and depends on the website goals. For example, if your intention is to rank for keywords and convert the residual traffic into conversions, long tail keywords is your best bet. On the other hand, if you aim to get eye balls on your content or website, although they are harder to rank for, broad match and generic keywords are best.

As you can see, the importance of keywords to a website largely depends on the website goals. Nevertheless, here are a few reasons why keyword research is such an important part of SEO.

Optimization

Throughout the last few chapters of this book, we have looked at various on-page and site wide optimization techniques. All webpage and content optimization starts at keyword research. In fact, as we have seen, to rank, you must employ exact match keywords and related keywords to your title tags and all the other key strategic areas we have looked at.

Keywords assist search engines in succinctly determining what your website covers/is all about. For example, using your keywords in your permalink URL and title tags can make a huge difference on your website ranking.

Additionally, using keywords for your non-text media ensures that search engines relate that media to your intended keywords. This makes it easier for your page/content to climb up the ranking ladder.

Competitiveness analysis

Keyword research allows you to learn and determine the popularity of specific keyword phrases and related phrases. For example, by using your keyword research tool, it is easy to determine which long tail keywords you should target depending on your end goal.

As indicated earlier, some keywords do not provide easy ranking opportunities. Keyword research allows you some insight into which keywords you should target in accordance with their competitiveness.

Proper keyword research and analysis allows you a chance to improve your ranking. For example, if you have an acne cures site, targeting the term acne as your main keyword may present a ranking challenge. However, by performing proper keyword research, it is easier for you to determine which easy to rank for keyword relate to acne. You can then use these keywords in your copy and website to improve on your ranking.

Targeting

Integrating keywords into your website allows you a chance to target a specific target audience. For example, if 'how to make money freelancing' is your keyword, it means that your target audience is someone looking to make money as a freelancer. While this information may not seem helpful, it is very central to how you write and optimize your copy.

Remember that keywords are search phrases used by users to search for information. By targeting specific keywords, you are targeting certain audiences.

Unfortunately, there is a huge misconception that keyword research is one of the hardest parts of SEO. To some extent, this notion is true. However, proper understanding of keyword research, how to do it, and how to use keywords on your website should make keyword research easier. Let us do that now.

How to do Keyword Research for a Better Google Ranking

Although Google ranking criteria has changed over time, one of the key factors that remain consistent is the use of keywords in determining ranking. This makes keyword research a very important undertaking.

Like everything else SEO related, there are many ways to perform keyword research. How you approach it depends on your targeted niche and audience. Nevertheless, here are some key steps you should go through when performing keyword research.

Step 1: Brainstorm and list down important and relevant topics and keywords related to your site

The process of keyword research always starts at brainstorming. When we talk about brainstorming, we mean you have to think about and list down topics and keywords related to the topic you intend to rank for. Ideally, go for about 5-10 topics or keywords.

Relevant topics and keywords are the most popular and frequently used topics or keywords. One of the ways you can do this is by using the alphabet soup method (also known as Google instant).

The alphabet soup method is where you head to Google, type in your relevant keyword or topic, and then add the letters of the alphabet after the phrase. For example, if we use the acne example, we would go to Google, type acne then the letter A B…. This will prompt Google to bring up frequent acne searches starting with the letter A or B, etc. To create your list of 5-10 topics or relevant keywords, go through all the letters of the alphabet. For example, using our acne example and the alphabet soup method, our topics would be:

- Acne antibiotics
- Acne body wash
- Acne cream

Do this for the keywords or topics you intend rank for and you'll have a ton of relevant keywords and topics to work with.

Step 2: Expand your list

Equipped with your keyword list from step one above, you now need to expand your topics and keywords lists. The second step in keyword research is very important in that it gives you an opportunity to identify easy-to-rank for keywords related to your site and your list of 5-10 key keywords or topics.

When expanding your list, ensure to restrict your searches to the most relevant keywords users are searching for. For example, if we take the last keyword in our list above Acne cream, I would expand this by placing myself in the shoes of online searches and coming up with related terms such users would be searching for. For instance:

- How to apply acne cream
- Where to buy acne cream
- Which is the best acne cream

You get the drift…

While this step may seem irrelevant, it is a key step in that it helps you create a sort of brain dump of searches potential clients and target audience are making. While the list you create will not be your final keyword list, it will give you a firm understanding on which key areas of your niche you should target.

Another way to drill down on your list is by using your website itself. If your website is already ranking for specific keyword phrases, you can use a keyword tool such as Google Analytics to drill down on related keywords or topics.

Step 3: Perform in-depth analysis on related terms, topics and keywords

If you're having trouble with step one and two, step three should make things a bit easier. Depending on your niche or topic, head over to Google and type something people interested in that topic may search for. For example, if your niche is how to do SEO, head over to Google and type how to do SEO. At the bottom of SERP page, there should be other related searches such as how to do SEO yourself, how to do SEO for your website, etc.

Searches related to how to seo

how to seo **your website**   how to **do** seo

how to seo **a website for free**   how to seo **your site**

how to seo **wordpress**   how to seo **your wordpress site**

how to seo **your blog**   how to seo **youtube**

1 2 3 4 5 6 7 8 9 10   **Next**

The related search options is an ideal way to zero in on other keywords your target audience may be using to search for information related to the keywords you aim to rank for.

Step 4: Identify and differentiate between generic keywords (head terms) and long tail keywords

Earlier on, we looked at different types of keywords. We also looked at which ones are easier and harder to rank for. In step four, categorize your growing keyword list into head terms and long tail keywords. Remember that generic keywords are often very vague and are often 1-3 words in length.

Aim to have a healthy mix of long tail keywords and head terms. This is so that you can have a well-balanced keyword strategy geared towards easy and fast ranking and traffic as well as long-term ranking and traffic.

Step 5: Spy on your competitors to know the keywords they are ranking for and how they are using these keywords you intend to rank for

Keywords hold special meaning to each webmaster. Understanding the keywords competing sites are ranking for is another important part of your keyword SEO strategy.

Your competitor could be ranking for keywords you can rank for, or keywords that hold little importance to you. By analyzing which keywords your competitors are ranking for, if these keywords are on your keyword list, you can optimize your content and website for these keywords.

Moreover, competitor analysis allows you some insight into which keywords your competitor is ignoring. You can then use this information to create optimized content or pages that help your overall ranking.

Competitions analysis will help you understand which head terms may be too difficult to rank for due to stiff competition and long tail keywords that may be easy picking. The trick to this is to have a healthy mix of long tail keywords and generic keywords geared towards creating a list that provides quick traffic and ranking benefits and those that provide long term ranking and authority for your website.

There are many ways to know which keywords competitors are ranking for. For instance, many paid keyword research tools allow you to use your competitors' domain to analyze which keywords are driving the most traffic to that specific site.

Step 6: Cut down your list using a keyword research tool

Step one through to five takes care of the raw part of keyword research. In step six, which is the final step, you need to narrow down your mix of keywords.

Using your raw keyword data, you need to eliminate or find variations for those keywords that are too competitive or that have little to no search data. For this, you need a keyword research tool.

A keyword research tool is a tool geared towards showing digital marketers the number of searches each keyword receives on a monthly basis. You can use many free and paid keyword research tools to slice down your keyword list. Tools such as Google Planner are very effective in showing traffic estimates and search volumes for specific keywords you may be considering.

While cutting down on your keyword list, make a point of eliminating all keywords that may have a ton of search volume data.

At this particular point, using the six-step process above, you should have a healthy mix of keywords ready for implementation and optimization on your website. Here is the thing though: although keywords are very important, simply finding the most profitable ones will not guarantee you easy ranking.

What will guarantee you easy ranking is how well you optimize those keywords into your content and page.

In the next chapter, we shall look at using keywords in your content and how to create content that users and search engine fall in love with.

Publishing Quality Content

Today, search is semantic. When we talk of search being semantic, what we really mean is that search engines today are all about providing quality to their end users. To them, this means providing their users with high quality, relevant content driven towards meeting the audience demands depending on their query.

A long time ago, search was not semantic. This made it possible for websites to stuff keywords in their content compromising readability and helpfulness for the end user. This also made it possible for unrelated sites to rank for unrelated search queries (a porn site ranking for acne cure or an electronic ecommerce site ranking for 6 pack workouts, etc.).

Today, content is one of the most important SEO ranking factors. Because search engines have evolved over time, today, they are able to use different factors to determine if our content is high quality.

For example, Google uses bounce rate to know how much time users are spending on your pages. When Google notices that users are not staying very long on your site, it assumes that the reason for this is that you're publishing crappy posts.

Today, search engines are all about providing the most relevant answers to their users. For example, when you search Google for pizza, instead of the SERP page starting with a Wikipedia page explaining the meaning of pizza, it starts with Pizza Hut because it assume you're interested in buying a pizza.

Note: The process of optimizing pages to a certain Geo location is called local SEO. It follows the same principal as normal SEO only that it's keyword research and optimization is targeted at a specific Geo location.

There is more than one reason why you should create high quality content. Other than the fact that search engines use content quality to determine where to rank pages on their index, content adds value to the target audience life. Content drives digital marketing. If you create crappy content, even if you were to use all the optimization tricks we looked at earlier, i.e. optimized permalinks, alt tag, long post, title tags, heading tags, etc., you would still fail to rank because that content was optimized for search engines and not for humans.

The importance of quality cannot be overstated. Unfortunately, quality is relative. In fact, what makes content great is something many marketers don't agree.

How To Write Great, Quality, SEO Friendly Content That Ranks On Google

<u>Be original</u>

Google loves original. However, even though Google loves original, you should create original, thought provoking, and intuitive, well-researched, long and well-written content with media not because Google loves it, but because your target audience loves it. Google analyzes all website. When you plagiarize work from the internet, even though Google may not punish you instantly, once the search bots realize that your content is plagiarized, they give credence to the site that published the content first (Google has also stated that they punish pages containing plagiarized content).

Creating original posts and pages is the easiest and yet the hardest thing. Here is why. Original is relative. There are those who believe that original means something no one else has thought of (which is highly unlikely), and then there are those who believe that creating original content is all about creating helpful content. Both these schools of thought are ok. Creative content is indeed sometimes something no one has thought of. However, sometimes, it is also about writing something that everyone has written about from a different perspective or in a different way.

To be original with your content, aim to provide your audience with the most relevant answer to their question. For example, if someone searches for "natural acne creams" lands on your page titled: *yourdomainname.com/naturalcnecures/5-natural-acne-cures-you-should-try/,* your content should provide the answer to that query. The content you create has to inspire something in your users.

Great, original copies compel users to take action. This action could be commenting (perhaps because the copy was thought provoking, irritating, funny, etc), the action could be a purchase (if the copy convinced them that certain product was what they were looking for), or it could be a social share because that content was very inspiring.

Create great, optimized, user/search friendly headlines

Allow me to ask you a question; when you access your email inbox, which emails do you read first? Digital marketing research shows that majority of people are drawn towards and are more inclined to click on creative headlines. This principle also holds true in print media and that is why the front-page headline on every newspaper is always something catchy that compels people to buy the paper.

Apply the same principle to your content. When creating content, toy around with a few titles. Roll them around to see which ones sound better and use the best. As a rule, aim to create headlines that feature your keywords in the first three words of the titles.

Use Keywords

Most digital marketers are quick to dispense the importance of weaving keywords into their content. Don't get me wrong; when we talk of using keywords within your content, we don't mean that you should have the keywords you want to rank for after every five words of content. No, doing this will prompt Google to punish you.

Instead, what we mean is that even though you should aim to have your keywords appearing at strategic points within your content, you should not use them if their use compromises content quality.

Google is all about quality and relevance. Although it is not a mandatory practice, aim to have the keywords you aim to rank for in the first 100 words of your content.

Create Sharable Content

Social networks are a big part of the world we live in today. Your copies should be alive to this fact. Sharable content is content that leaves a reader with a question. It is content that is interesting and compelling to read, content that tells a story by using a catchy and promising introduction. This is content that users can share with their friends on social media, email, etc.

Sharable content also means content that communicates better using non-text media. Research shows that images, videos, diagrams, etc. are better at illustrating a point. Moreover, most people hate reading blocks of texts. Make a point of using images and videos in your content. Moreover, make a point of using alt tags to tell search engines what your site and media covers.

Another key thing to consider when creating sharable content is creating content that is pointed and short. Short in this case does not mean focusing on word count. It means creating comprehensible content grouped into easy to read and navigate paragraphs.

Linking Strategy - Google Link Building Guide For Beginners

One of the key criteria Google uses to rank websites is the number of inbound links pointing to a particular piece of content or page, and the number of outbound links from that page pointing to other quality websites.

In Google ranking, Link building is not a new concept. In fact, link building has been as much a part of SEO as everything else we have looked at. Don't believe me? Go back into the echelons of search history and you will realize that there was a brief time when link spamming (having many spammy, irrelevant sites pointing back to your site) was enough to give you first page ranking.

Before we outline the importance of link building, it is only right that we understand what link building really is. Let's do that now.

What Is Link Building?

Link building covers two key areas: outbound and inbound links. Outbound links are informative inks that link from your content to other related content on the internet. They may include links to relevant sources, links to media such as infographics and videos, download links etc.

Inbound links on the other hand are links that point back to your website i.e. someone uses your link in the same manner you would use an outbound link. A link in this case is a navigational path that a user can use to jump from one place to the other on the World Wide Web.

Linking is very important because search engines use links to crawl the web and your pages. Quality link building is one of the hardest bits in SEO. On the other hand, link building is a learnt art. It requires a bit of ingenuity on your part. Unfortunately, like everything else search engine optimization we have looked at, no two link building strategies or campaigns are similar and exact in every way. This can make it relatively hard for marketers to build links that Google falls in love with.

Although there are many ways to build links, and despite the fact that there are many types of link acquisitions, below are the main/basic types of links.

1- Natural links- Natural links are links whereby other webmasters naturally link back to your pages or content. These types of links require very little work on your part other than the creation of quality content that other users can link back to.

2- Manual links- Manual links are also known as outreach links. They involve manually reaching out to other webmaster for links, submitting your site to directories, etc. These types of links are a bit difficult to achieve because as you reach out to other webmasters and bloggers, you have to offer them value preposition, i.e. outline the advantages of that site linking back to you.

3- Self-created links- Self-created links are links you create yourself. For example, if you are a member of a specific forum, or comment often on certain blogs, you have the opportunity to create links. Google does not favor self-created links and often penalize sites that pursue this linking strategy.

Depending on your end goals, there are many ways to create natural links that integrate well into your content and add value to your ranking. Although the internet is not lacking in this department, here is how to create a ranking strategy that works.

How To Build A High, Quality Back-Links Strategy That Google Loves

Today, Google concentrates on high quality natural links. This means building links to you should no longer be about posting your website URL all over the internet in the hopes that this will increase your ranking. To build the authority of your site using back links, do the following:

Get links from High quality sites

As we keep on stating, Google is all about quality. Long gone are the days when a ton of back links was all it took to rank.

Today, search engines have evolved and now understand the difference between high quality links and low quality, spammy links. If you can get links from high quality sites in your niche or field of business, they can boost your ranking tremendously. For example, if you have a social media marketing company and website, you can inquire about contributing content to an authority site such as socialmediaexaminer.com, in exchange for a back link.

The key to this is making sure that you're adding value to the main site by writing quality content optimized for people and search engines as well.

When building links, avoid spammy links that add zero value to your content, audience, website, or business. If you're unsure about which links to pursue, you can spy on your competitors using certain tools to know which sites they link to and which sites link to them.

Get social

Search engines are very keen on social signal. They love content that is being shared socially. Social media will not only be good for your social signals, it is also an important avenue for marketing your brand, getting the right eyeballs on your content, and connecting with network marketing.

Create a social media strategy that clearly defines how you will use social media to engage with your community, which social media platform you shall concentrate on and, your intended results.

Concentrate on creating natural links

Regardless of whether you are creating inbound or outbound links, all your links should be natural. Natural in this case means that if you're creating outbound links to helpful sites, they should fall naturally within your content. The same applies to inbound links. If an authority site offers you the opportunity to contribute to their community with your content, ensure to link back in your writer bio or link back to your site within the content in a natural manner that provides value for the user.

Webmaster Tools

At this point, you have everything you need to make Google fall in love with your website and send you a ton of traffic. We have looked at how to prepare your website for success by doing proper on page-SEO. We have also seen how different areas of site wide optimization can affect your ranking (and seen what you need to do to nail down your site wide optimization). We have also seen how to do keyword research, create SEO optimized content that other sites link back to. Even though we have done very well, there is still one more thing we have not learnt: webmaster tools.

What is Google Search Console?

What we refer to as Google search console is what we formerly referred to as Google webmaster, which was rebranded to Google search console on May 20 2015. Google search console is a tool Google provides to webmasters to help them optimize their website for search visibility and check site-indexing status.

Although Google search console serves many purposes, some of the key elements it helps webmaster with include; submitting a sitemap, analyzes your SEO efforts and other key areas that are effective for first page ranking.

Google webmasters tools are the essential SEOs samurai sword. The webmaster tool is a tool that every digital marketer should aim to utilize to measure how well all the SEO work he or she has put into their website has paid off. The webmaster tools allow you to know which of your optimized content or pages are doing well, which of your keywords are bringing in the most traffic, etc.

How to use the Webmaster Tool

Google is all in one. If you have a Gmail account, signing up for webmasters tool is easy. Simply sign in to your Gmail account and then access the webmasters tools. If you haven't used search console before, you'll have to add your site to the console.

After this, you'll have to add your site and verify it in the webmaster tools. Today, the verification process is very easy and you can do it with the mere click of a Google pop up. Depending on your hosting, you may also have to include a Meta tag to your homepage or upload a HTML file to your hosting root folder. You can also confirm ownership of your site through Goggle analytics if you already have it installed.

After creating your account or login into your account, add all site versions. This is especially useful because if you fail to do it, webmaster may neglect to show or illustrate critical issues that may make crawling your site harder. In terms of adding all domains, you should also make a point of adding all subdomains and root domains.

The whole reasoning behind Google search console is that it allows you to see your website as Google sees it. Occasionally, the console will send you site messages notifying you whenever there are important issues that need your attention. Whenever you get a site message, ensure to take care of the problems that arise. Often times, this may be malware alerts, crawl errors, sitemap errors, etc. Nevertheless, you should note that even though Google strives to ensure that you get the most important updates in a timely manner, there could be a delay between when the problem manifests and the time Google notifies you.

5 Google Search Console Tips Guaranteed To Improve Your SEO

Make use of Search Queries

Once you connect your site to the search console, you will notice the Search Queries section. This section will always show your ranking for your keywords as well as indicate organic search impressions and CTR (click through rates) for all your keywords (segmented by keyword).

The search queries section will allow you to see how your SEO campaign is fairing over time and allow you to toggle to Google trends. You can use the search queries section to discover which keywords are performing better in search, which ones are driving keywords to your website, and which ones are low hanging (easy to rank for).

Make use of traffic patterns

Other than providing you with the average position for all your top search queries/keywords driving traffic to your site, the webmaster tool also allows you insight into the average ranking position for specific pages on your website including posts. This allows you amazing insight into; which content and keywords are performing better, click through rate for each particular page, and all content with low average ranking but great CTR.

Using this, you can adjust the Meta description on your content (optimize it) to get better CTR or concentrate on link building quality links to content that is not ranking very well. This data is especially important in helping you identify which content performs better with your target audience and search engines. For instance, if your longer content performs better on SERP and your target audience, you can concentrate on creating longer SEO optimized posts.

View individual keyword insights

As we have seen repeatedly, 80% of all organic traffic starts at a search engine and thus the need for webmasters to optimize their website and content for search. The console allows you insight into the performance of individual keywords. This feature allows you to see data into which pages or content on your website is ranking better or performing better in search. To view the keyword insight data, while on the Search queries table, select the keywords you aim to check. This information is very helpful in that it allows you to know which pages Google thinks are extremely relevant to your website and how they relate to the keywords you're targeting. If you find that specific keywords on one of your popular pages or articles are performing better in search, you can then create content around these keywords or their natural variations.

Use authorship statistics

Google search console is much more than a raw data platform confined to your site. The Google Authorship section available in the labs section of the search console allows you to view your authorship statistics that shows statistics for all and any external post that you've been verified as the author.

Although this feature may seem moot, it allows you insight into which content is generating more views, as well as insight into how that piece of content is performing in search. This can make coming up with new content ideas easy. For instance, if a guest post you authored for an authority or popular site about a topic of interest is performing better in terms of click through, and search ranking, you can curate content related to that post.

Use site speed metrics

How fast or slow your website and webpages load is one of the key factors Google uses to rank websites. Moreover, rumor has it that the Hummingbird update now prioritizes mobile page load speed as part of its ranking criteria.

The Google search console allows you to track how fast or slow it takes the Bots at Google to download your content/page. Although google page speed also offers the same insight and their remedies, using this metric in webmasters tool is an excellent way to test your page speed at a page level. You can access this Webmaster feature by accessing the crawl menu within your console and select fetch as Google. After this, enter the URL you aim to fetch and allow Google a chance to do its thing. The results should display your site load speed. If your site load speed is anywhere below 500 milliseconds, this is ok. However, anything above this will cause a drag in load time, which will increase your bounce rate.

SEO Dangers - Google SEO Mistakes You Should Avoid

Optimizing your website for Google and other search engines is not an exact science. Despite having covered everything Google and everything else you can do to tweak different features of your website and content to rank better, it is very common to find many webmasters making common SEO mistakes that end up costing them valuable ranking points.

Although there are many Google SEO mistakes you should avoid, below are the most common ones and their dangers to your ranking.

Keyword stuffing

Earlier on, we mentioned that keyword stuffing days are way past behind us. Keyword stuffing speaks directly to the heart of SEO: quality content. If you use keywords after every five words, you will compromise the readability and quality of your great and original copy. Keyword stuffing is something Google frowns upon and discourages vehemently.

Instead of keyword stuffing your content or webpage, optimize your keywords on page and site wide. Use keywords in your meta tags and meta descriptions, as well as permalinks. Remember that the deliberate repetition of key phrases within your content or page will not mean better ranking. It will instead mean penalties that drive you further down the ranking index.

Un-original, plagiarized copies

Some people will be quick to point out that nothing in this world is truly original. However, as we saw earlier, Google loathes those who plagiarize. Google loves original copies. So much so that it will reward you with a ton of organic traffic if you create SEO optimized copies.

The rule of thumb here is to ensure that you are providing value to your target audience, by educating, inspiring, informing, entertaining them, etc.

Google also hates duplicate content. Duplication in this case could mean duplicate content on your website. Content duplication on your site can happen in a number of ways. For example, duplicate content that appears in more than one location on your website. This type of duplication is negatively potent to your SEO strategy because it confuses the search engine to a point (search engine gets confused about which content to index). This can lead to a drop in search rankings.

If you must have duplicate content on your website/page, use 301 redirects that redirect from lower pages to your preferred web page.

Use of ambiguous titles tags, and Meta descriptions

Title tags and Meta descriptions are a very important part of on-page and site-wide optimization as we saw earlier. Many webmasters fail to give their pages or content unique titles and Meta descriptions.

Title tags, and Meta descriptions should be unique and reflect the uniqueness and content contained within a website. Moreover, as we indicated earlier, use keyword in your titles and Meta descriptions.

Spammy or paid backlinks

Search engines have evolved a lot over time. Today, as we saw in the linking chapter of our book, search engines can differentiate between earned, quality links and low, quality spammy links.

When creating your link building strategy, target high quality inbound and outbound links that add value to the target audience. For example, rather than join a thousand and one forums and link back to your site from your BIO, creating high quality guest posts for authority sites would work better for SEO purposes.

Moreover, although Google does not explicitly state what they do to sites that pursue the paid link option, many digital marketers agree that buying links is not something you should consider.

Failure to measure

Search engine optimization is not an exact science. As such, getting it right requires a lot of experimentation; tweaks, re-implementation and re-tweaks. After implementing your SEO strategy, you need to track if your SEO efforts are paying, which keywords and pages are working best and how your site is performing. All this is impossible without the use of Google Webmasters tools and Google analytics.

Conclusion

Today, Google search is all about providing its users with the most relevant results for their queries. By doing keyword research, you can know search terms users are using. By doing keyword research, you can also understand which questions or keywords hold more value to your target audience. Using this information, you can then create useful, original content that Google and your audience will love. Moreover, by optimizing your content and website using the on-page, site-wide, and off-page optimization knowledge we have accumulated so far, you can bet your page, content or website will climb up the search index to number one.

Thank you again for purchasing this book!

I hope this book was able to help you to understand the different aspects of SEO.

The next step is to implement what you've learnt and grow your traffic to a level you've never known before.

Thank you and good luck!

37378384R00031

Printed in Great Britain
by Amazon